The grass is greener over your grave

Other books by the author

**Poetry**
*Lyre*
*Opera*
*Edge Music*

**Translation**
Gianni Siccardi, *The Blackbird*
*George Dyuŋgayan's Bulu Line: a West Kimberley song cycle*

**Criticism**
(co-edited with Peter Denney) *Transcultural Ecocriticism: global, romantic and decolonial perspectives*
*Speaking the Earth's Languages: a theory for Australian-Chilean postcolonial poetics*

# The grass is greener over your grave

## Stuart Cooke

PUNCHER & WATTMANN

© Stuart Cooke 2023

This book is copyright. Apart from any fair dealing for the purposes of study and research, criticism, review or as otherwise permitted under the Copyright Act, no part may be reproduced by any process without written permission. Inquiries should be made to the publisher.

First published in 2023
Published by Puncher & Wattmann
PO Box 279
Waratah NSW 2298

info@puncherandwattmann.com

A catologue record for this book is available from The National Library of Australia.

ISBN    9781922571755

Cover design by Miranda Douglas

Printed by Lightning Source International

# Contents

  9 Shore
10 Extension
12 In Memory
16 On the Path above a Village
18 Cape York
20 This is what you have done for me

## First

23 Coastal, as in Galactic
26 Feed
29 Saving the Rainforest
32 Sunburnt
34 Extending the Blue Track
36 Blade
38 Wander in &/Under
39 Intertown
41 Isla Negra Ode
43 Storm
45 Tierra Weather
46 Deep Dive
51 Hidden
55 Wagga to Coast

## Field Notes

63 Fade, Into
67 The Trees
69 Old World
71 Sutherland
72 Upon the Tongue of a Valley's Enormous Mouth
74 yellow:
75 Branch

77 Some More Thoughts on the Rainforest

## South-East

 81 Hinterland
 83 Black Rocks
 85 Late World, Humid
 87 Verge
 89 Song of the Wandering Cat
 94 Cabo Polonio
 96 Laguna
 98 South-East
100 Partial, & Remorse
102 Wollombi

105 Notes
106 Acknowledgements

In memory of Martin Harrison (1949-2014)
Poet, Essayist, Teacher

# Shore

*after Martin Harrison, after Michel Deguy*

The rhyme is a silver lake.
The raven leaves a nova in your arms.
When I wrote, buds
of music bloomed in your reading.

There's no escape,
no one else will understand.
My sky collapses
on fields of withered flowers.

I return to speak with a drum
of your death; the only reply
(the years are dwindling coppice)
is a call from the deep.

Someone kicks a stone in the street.
I am falling, what
if the rain could fall,
make your grave green in my arms.

# Extension

no beginning but the channel's silvery plain shooting into middle distance
to be cut off by the river, its resolute monotony,
lapping and lapping back

domed here by a thin bank of sand,
this wide, friendly channel, glazed with limp shreds of light, sluiced with dinghies,
hemmed by fenced yards,
its clouded-up windiness, the tufts and textures of a low, inner sky,
and (far off) a front's caught on the hinterland, you feel it bubbling and blustering
(there'll be rain later, it'll frizz and spit and pass)

it's the channel's glazed, glutinous consistency,
how it's shorn from the scratched river (passing silently in the distance),
how light can't grasp it, can't take hold,
spilling from the rims of clouds, how light collides with the weather-beaten river,
scrawls over it wildly, skids towards me,
finds no purchase on the channel's polished mauve then sprays out, torn up and scattering
across this glowing, fidgeting grass,
this is how you echo inside me,
here where I came to search for you (here, as it's funnelled from out there)

(out there) the sun's misty rays shot through clouds, now disappearing behind the range,
the dark, forested wetness of the distance paired
with the dried-out banksia cones sprinkled around me,
with an earth pocked with ant mounds,
with fragments of bark and twig that press and imprint themselves upon my legs,
and banana palms glistening, and a lonely flag with an absurd, souvenir shop blueness,
a faded redness (and that crescendo, slowly building, the sting
of an ant bite, the swipe)

I stand up and the grass tips into the sand,
the sand bank slides into the water,
then I'm poured over the channel and across the river to the other side, onward,
over the houses (further back),
on towards the hinterland and those smeared, watery blooms of cloud,
the sudden, overwhelming proximity of it,
the background transformed completely into rain front, mist scape,
until moments later it clears again, leaving the mountains to re-draw themselves,
to re-contour their sub-tropical darkness with saddles and tree clusters

I've used these same words before, and you've used these words before,
we've used all of these words before,
the channel's leaden solution flattens the sand into a leathery band, and in the distance,
back beyond the river, a glimpse of road,
a road threaded by an occasional car (the river moves almost as fast):
assemblage of a late summer's storm, its depth, its inevitability,
and this grass scattered with banksia leaves, their rusty commas through greenness,
their flesh-brown curls like some kind of fried street food from far off,
the way these leaves—
the way the sun breaks out now into complete, drumming presence
and burns the channel into invisible spectra,
the invisible, knowing it's there, a storm's forehead nudged by a blustering southerly,
it comes anyway, regardless of knowing,
the cool noon sinking into a humid afternoon,
the way it can overwhelm you, the way it overwhelmed you,
how the lines appear with their impervious smoothness,
even as the clouds unravel, and what they say is lost—

## In Memory

… this circle which I do not form, which forms me, this coiling over of the visible upon the visible… if I was able to understand how this wave arises within me, how the visible which is yonder is simultaneously my landscape, I can understand *a fortiori* that elsewhere it also closes over upon itself and that there are other landscapes besides my own.

—Maurice Merleau-Ponty

—now, a lens twists light / to burn this life:

(those idle waters
around your island, their
unreachable interval)

you are like a cay piled with silicate,
a cay brushed with scrub
and knobbed by a dense copse:
your most striking feature is your shady mind,
its patience with the sun.

\*

(I blame the ocean
as much as I hide in it.
I think ahead of myself to death
but I am recalled by featureless prospect,
by the end of thinking.
I watch as a canal steadily tears
through a continent's scalp.)

\*

How can we write
of a life spent thinking
through sound?

Planes scraped the heavens with your elsewheres,
before you screeched, in a raucous flame of sulphur,
across the frosted harbour.

(in which mineral?)
(in whose coppered pages?)

\*

This might be you: a lanky heron balancing on a gate.

This might be you: three bronzed bodies
stroking out beyond the break.

Will the land speak to us of your speaking?
(perhaps as a breeze through grass
translated into shards of wriggling light,
a post-impressionist haze, briefly chilled
then laid flat and stretched
into feathery, furtive strokes)

Burgundy wing threading the ridges together,
swarms of staves around the tips of things,
quatrains of wheel and being
and mark and breath congealing in silent choir,
the vale's glazed in solar fervour, you step off the threshold into presence,
what do you see, what do you see—

\*

I blame my self and my childhood for not knowing,
I cannot inhabit you for more than a moment;
what do you see, as this waits and this takes off,
as the flesh fills with time, becomes pure movement, its pulsing, its humbled, hesitant spilling,
as it hobbles back into shape;
vagrant yet docile compositions, who will see the dimensions
of your flaking map?

\*

After the funeral, I walk around your home and search for you inside me
(language, like peeling bark, falls from my body);
I cannot live this life, I cannot complete you,
I cannot be your person.

I imagine the hue of my blood
and its useless art on the ground
(I doubt that, beyond this,
I'd have much else).

\*

Hidden near the shore, just beyond the rise,
in the shade of the crouched banksia,
in the dim rivers of sunlight that tangle into steaming pools

(images ascend like curling kites into chiselled blueness)

a traveller's eye knots with the long facts of wood song

(where vision begins, back here)

(here
is the distance, venturing)

\*

—the birth of love at dawn, to be logged by afternoon,
its great muscle left thumping inside the evening's gnarled barrel,
what shining capsule—speeding across a bridge—
what hysterical utterance came racing from your grey moors

(it propels you deeper)
as you waited by the river and thought of who you'd blamed,
of the night, the night, and your clutching (on the other side,
caliginous figures hover over a curious tide),
your senses swept into your reaching,
until what you sought was overwhelmed by what you were:

desert flooding from the caves beneath a cliff,
a pallid shape inscribing sky with noisy forest,
and each of your questions resting,
like the moon's spilt milk, on a lover's skin

the night, the river, the bridge,
your body stiffening like a cay
as it draws itself with an ocean
(what do you say?
as the universe trembles and collects itself
in the dark shelter of your mouth)
—body full of grace, there, compelled to the verge of flight

## On the Path above a Village

I've risen from the flood
of wind through the valley on a trail
through meadow, history bunched up
in remnant clumps of glittering hay.

If I walk like you through this resting country,
will I recall what you saw, echo your sight?
Sun pushed back by a knoll,
will I find what you left, waiting?

Hint of a voice from behind the summit, then
the bees and their lost violins.
A stand of pine huddles
through a sheep's brilliant skull.

Your vase could be atop any one of these crests
or sequestered down an abandoned shaft.
I try not to think of you wheezing
like a beetle at my feet.

Across the paddock of the sky:
wispy husks of words.
In this cool, aching ray (slipped
from crevice, slipping

from curve), in a boulder's grizzled brain
or in the cicadas' last tower,
do I see the circle?
do I hear its polished note?

A beryl snake of wine coils around my leg,
I watch the vibrations bake into whiteness
—even after all of time, I will not find you—
I hear them trickle through a subterranean pipe.

## Cape York

When you arrive at the tip of the Cape, the coast
accelerates to the liminal and its laminate lifts. You splinter
into the rivulets left by an outgoing tide, your translucent threads
untangling into a turquoise open, where jungle inflates into gentle mountains,
your vision dilating along the shore's pixelated arc, or swerving
to pool in paper-deep lakes for when the breeze comes, building,
now blustering, eager, chopping up the water
into thousands of flickering marks.
You're swept along the curve until its milky wand finally vanishes
beneath a headland's elegant limb,
leaving your gaze to slide towards the ridge, which floats into ash
flecked with apple, the silhouette of a dream-form, an opaque taipan
full with a feed, resting her head where ocean bends
into sky, this inmost signal of the moment's breadth, the way you step into it
as it comes soaring back, soaring over the mast
of the yacht rocking imperceptibly in the bay,
as it subsumes your questions in its salty cry,
as it reappears from within them, like your love for those
who have walked on while you've stopped to watch,
who have become tiny, ebony scratches in that immensity of sapphire firmament,
have drawn you into the outside and laughed with you there,
have left you exposed, like a hermit without
his shell, to certain dangers, but also to the gaps
in nets of code, into which you might nestle, if only for a second,
before this surge fills you completely,
this compression of infinite space and its mad, fricative operas
into the sand's long monopoly, watch it racing towards you,
its stiff chord obliterating the possibility of anything but presence,
this ardent, unrumpled animal lumbering through you,
leaving you rattled.

But the mangroves are waiting patiently,
the foreground's sprouted with their gnarled snorkels,
as if huge, ligneous lungs lay breathing below—
what place finds you? what place knows?
There's a fragile bone that runs thin as a hair round the bend
then extends into the skeleton of all that is happening,
despite that *never*, the what might never be,
because of the opaque crust of a body, of its whisper
and hover, how you can peer briefly beneath,
but how you will sink as space begins to stretch,
when you walk towards her with desire splitting your chest,
when you feel the impending closeness, of that choir, of matter unfolding,
memory's colossal bass riddled with tropical winds,
with forests of lives, how could you have known this?
how could you have known?

## This is what you have done for me

This is what I would do, as the sun sheathes itself in a bank of clouds,
this northern country dried out by late afternoon, then its breathy dryness breaking open,
a wedge of the top end soaked again with frenetic squalls,
this is what I would do for you,
as the headlands nudge a shallow, rounded ocean,
its immovable stillness, basis for horizon,
a stillness uplifted by wave after wave, these layers of
consciousness rippling with currents, with trains of sets, I would turn to you,
the two of us seated together on the sand,
exhausted after our days of travel and exploration,
seated together on this beach at the tip of Australia,
our theories buried in endless, exuberant country as it rushes past us,
as it drifts, as it holds us at night,
finally we have seen what Olsen brought to the cities,
fillets of languid pindan unrolling from the windscreen,
short wires of fern and pandanus, wiry reeds of skipping earth,
silt shots and parrot streaks, pocked explosions of lime and hive thronging near heaven level,
the cobalt crown over the shore's creamy sickle, the dozing crocs,
and vines sprawled over dunes, their paired leaflets, their buds,
then mauve flowerlets probing sunward, this neon penumbra, its flowering,
this is what I would tell you, of the distances, their physics going up in fireworks,
how they float and settle beside and before us,
to leave impressions on sand, on damp, soft ground,
their midget signatures fringing a vast screen of islands and palm cockatoos,
all of it stretched close to white and framed in drowsy blue,
until what we are starts to rotate slowly, like some stunning, circular verb
above a swelling, fluorescent river,
shocked with the static that webs us to the light.

First

## Coastal, as in Galactic

The moon is the first thing to notice, the first
to discard. We lean into a dark universe,

our legs blur beneath us, soon we can see it
from afar: our lost friends, our dying cities,

even the death of us. Some are jostling
like glittering pistons, lots are

wailing like open ovens. The limbs
of a poet are woven from the letters

of a nova, dumb and magnificent as any
convoluted scale. If we journey into the flesh

to where our rhythm was lost, the present
spins into a gourd, continents into chords,

into chords, melodies of ecologies
are strobed into disco, I want

to groove with you, groove with you,
the madness of the music is a planet,

the harmony is a web, we are strung into desires
that exceed us, there is a halo around the hole

in the centre of our allotment.
When I step out of the documentary

I'm confronted with a quadrant, I build a haiku.
Inside the poem I am safe, I play a trombone,

my life begins when it leaps,
I jump and we're alone. Only a painting

could frame your thicket, I want record
of my adoration, I will scrawl in dance.

When impression bursts with collective,
our crown of forests ignites, I coat my cells

in the ocean's crumbed plastic.
Where is the right position?

We crowd into the negative, we fade
into the valley of the voice. Has the story

come to an end? Where
were we going? Toward a crystallised

infinity, where we in fact are the other
we have been awaiting, and any glance

over the shoals of possibilities
that lie strewn by our globular record

is like gazing into a mirror reflecting the inner-
most depths of the soul. Often Truth is a lie,

the word conceals a mob, discarding
the void of Mind, I wade into the muck

between the marks, the interval mutters,
I press upon another, entangle with its

mass. To speak is to move, to bend, to be,
we tell as we're told, on a stage of gesture,

touch, retreat. I will finish the circle,
I will abandon narration, oration,

the body will lose its tone. Let me hear you by horn,
by failure, by flight. We are rush hour

along the freeways of a dying thesaurus,
the will is the music that frames us,

the body disappears when it stops.

# Feed

On the footpath, on the billboard,
I'm the smiling face, I represent my culture,
when I smile, I'm the source of my culture.
They glued me on to time,
they dressed me up in a glowing soul and pieces of a body.
To the north, I'm bounded by Islam;
to the south, by amnesia; from the east,
St. Paul comes sailing across the sea,
there's my polity; to the west,
I am open, or I'm completely impotent.

There I am in a satellite, revolving; I'm fluid.
Later I become aware of the earth, I walk the way you do, and you,
they nail me onto poles, onto billboards, all in one era.
High school I'm all the rage, they call me by a number, I loathe the hierarchy,
they put a sign on me that says *Man*, I laugh, strut, I'm constantly lurching,
I joke and poke. I'm here, there, checking in;
I'm in the aisle seat next to spirits
in Thriller jackets, *liking* things, remembering things, what's that? Oh,
I'm bored, now I'm disembarking, so many matches and special announcements,
somebody from the future is signalling me, I don't know what's good or what's evil.
At brunch my head came loose and floated away,
I'm hanging in the ether, in terror, or busting my pecs at the gym,
I'm stupefied with goals, numbers, smells, with emotions that have no emoticons,
I refuse to believe in any detailed dogma.

I'm unlike my forebears, I'm unlike you, and you, and me,
I stand on a horse with my beer, and sometimes I fall out on to the pavement in a brawl
with legends of the nation,
but later I'm with my nutty uncles, guffawing,
then back at the gym, working my glutes.

I'm on the other side of the planet a hundred days from now, joining Rio in church,
I'm desperate to be close, where can I hide my fear?
Nations of cinema samba on my cranium,
data, warheads, yoga,
photos droop over benches,
different weights and motions attract my attention,
I'm about to change my face, the year will reveal the truth, I will walk on Mars.

I'm bound to my birth and I border with agony.
I cackle like static in the noggins of ugly people, of intellectuals,
in your shadow's crappy shed.
Everything can become transparent,
other faces will appear beside mine, their brooding aquifers, their dribbled love,
newsfeeds that span to eternity will start to repeat themselves,
I'll mingle with science, kiss people at will, consider voodoo,
I'll insinuate my self into countless recesses.

Souls in despair, look on the bright side. Souls discontent, chill out!
I loathe those who define themselves, the contrarians and the worriers.
Long live Sundays and a selection of beverages and movies,
long live sacrifice, and mothers who are really mothers,
dudes who are really dudes.
Long live the transformed, who were perfect and then replicated or re-perfected themselves,
and me, my stateless, transcendent confusion.
The man I was 20 years ago is the prey of the man I am today,
of the women I've undressed.
Life is bodies splitting with summer, with grunge rhythms, engine rhythms, sampled rhythms,
and deserts quaking under the fingers of sex.
I subscribe to cuttings from suitable theories.

I'm at eye level and molecular, on billboards, proteins, surfboards,
in the wallets of young men, in the whims of millennials,
gestating in my Broadbeach studio, in the prayers of the hunters,
I'm merry and remorseless, my muscles burn, my ending's deferred
by faith's two-faced flame, watch it contorting, twisting and devouring itself,
I need you, my sticky little era, your jingle twinkling along the promenade
like the ribs of the Milky Way.

## Saving the Rainforest

i liquidated my portfolio and bought property in the peruvian amazon
i got a nice chunk next to the national park
i sold my apartment, left london
i wanted to save the rainforest, i could do it on my own

next i'm traipsing through a rabid city, sans Spanish, coughing on exhaust
sweat collects in the stiff gutter of my upper lip
i get a translator, we leave the city, he takes me to my new home
he'll help me with the old man i bought it from

when we get there, this old man, he's waiting out the front of the house, he says buenas tardes
he tells my translator, there's another guy, he lives nearby, he gets lumber from this land
so i tell my translator, tell this man, it's my land now and we can't have that
and the old man, he says, sí, and my translator says, yes sir i understand
and we're all on the same page, or so i thought

a couple of days later i see that guy the old man mentioned, he turns up in a rusty truck
he stops outside my front door, he says, hola, but my translator's in town
so i say, HOLA, and smile and point to my forest
WOOD? i ask, sí, he says
i nod sternly, what else can i do?

he comes back for more a week later but now I have my translator
you can't keep chopping down these trees, i tell him, i bought this plot from the old man, i live here now,
        we need to protect the selva
entiendo señor, pero mi familia, he understands, says the translator, but can he have some time to find
        other work?
okay, i say, but no more than a week, this has to end

but this guy keeps coming back, week after week, taking all the timber that'll fit on his old truck
i try to talk to him again but he starts coming in through the back way
that sly bastard, i think, that cheeky bugger, this has to stop

i take my translator and we pay him a visit
we go to his hut with its dirt yard, its dirty chickens pecking about
his wife and his daughter come out first, then he comes from around the side, wiping his hands with a rag
we have to talk, i say, bueno, he replies
we sit on some plastic chairs, a chicken pecks near my feet
coffee, señor? no, gracias, i say
I get ready to establish the parameters
but his daughter—what is she, 5 or 6? she's 9, says the translator—
she comes and taps me on the arm
her smile's so big it breaks my heart, as in, i can literally feel the organ tearing open
she's lovely, i say, es linda, dice, what's her name? Isobela
hola Isobela, i say, and it's like i've injected her with something, her face lights up even brighter and she claps like a firecracker
i ruffle her hair and she giggles and spins
hoolaaa, i say, while the mother and father sit there, smiling wanly
then i notice the girl's lips, and how her tongue is squeezed between them, and how she doesn't speak
        but grunts like a calf
nació normal, she was born a normal child, says the mother, whose voice sounds like a recording, whose eyes
        remain on the ground,
but when she was 3 months old i was working in the paddy, i had her with me like always, but then she fell
        out of my sling into the husker,
it spun her around so fast, her body was tossed so violently, i screamed and screamed,
i thought she was dead, we had to wait while someone turned off the machine,
by the time we got her out her brain was bleeding,
she needs constant care, she'll never work,
often i think about killing her before i kill myself

Isobela laughs like a chainsaw when I try to catch her, she is the happiest human in peru
they are waiting for me to speak but I chase her around the yard
we are in a clearing hacked out of a mammoth jungle
i try to ignore the clammy rent expanding in my chest
i can feel the buttery maggots pulsing in its ravine
i try to ignore them, i should wrap things up
but i am here now, and if what's open will close
i'll be stuck in it

# Sunburnt

What mead, what tillage! A fine grove
of shade and tranquillity crowds into the navy
of my eye,
the brown and the dim skied into otherwise,
whatever's seen, I cannot share it.

In my cerebellum I'm a photo of a mountain,
an exhausted nation where lust scorches plains
into ragged horizon, that border
dragged over the ranges, before which
all terror and all of its jewels are mine.

Here's the death: ring-barked wan
as the moon, tragic in my classic mist,
my tangled hush, my pen's hot gold coils.
I raze forests for verandas, where I pot exotic orchids,
I press death down, down into the south,
into dark, simmering soil.

This cored heart, cored country,
my pitiless eyes, sick of art.
What we see, we can bless: we watch
our cattle die, peel their hides
for the drums of our anthem's splatter,
our dead armies, our reflections,
our skulls of electric desire.

At my core is a cored country,
its scattered rhymes of rainbow
and reptile, oyster and fire; I stripped it
back threefold, from spirit
to serpent, serpent to parched
paddock, because while I gaze, I gaze,
I need a veil on which to rest my gaze.

An opal hearse awaits my lavish will
in a country that never loved me,
that I will not understand. My hopes
are hawks in search of splendours,
but my lucent vision's blind to its basis:
brown land, black law, the deaths I won't see,
whose songs I'll hear upon my own.

# Extending the Blue Track, Minyirr Park

*after Philip Hodgins*

We'd thought it would take a lot longer.
The early sun clapped
our backs as we trudged down there,
our shoes sinking into the pindan.

By the time we arrived,
the rangers had already unloaded the planks and ropes.
Fifteen or so were in a row, thick planks of pine
strung together with plastic rope and laid out
like long ladders.

We rolled them up and
lugged them up the path,
which was hard enough because you'd trip
on the planks that had been laid down already,
and in the gaps between them the sand was soft and unsteady.
And then the rolls would get caught on branches, or
on the posts that were stuck at intervals along the track.
The dunes were pretty steep, too,
and clustered like a squat range
along the kilometres of the beach.

We were happy to reach the top
where we'd hit the breeze coming in off the Indian.
It was a great view
but you didn't look at it much
because of how it taunted you, the thought
of swimming through cool water,
while your clammy shirt wrapped you up
and your hands stung with splinters.

It only took a few trips
to get all the rolls up to the top.
Then we had to go down and get more of the posts.
These were big but not so heavy; still,
your shoulders got pretty sore.
We made a ragged chain
up the dunes and passed them on to one another.

But that was all over soon enough
and we assembled up the top of the dunes for a rest.
Miklo told us a bit: we were on the first hill
the creation beings climbed when they came from the ocean
to roam out across the continent. He pointed
to other spots up the coast
where more came out and followed.
Turning back, we could see the outline of the new track
extending to the south;
in a couple of days, we'd have laid planks
along the lot of it.

## Blade

Monday morning, another Black death
                in custody, the angel emerging
                                    from misty firmament
                      her long, sooty howl

              I step out onto the earth
        and squint beneath the recollections
                                      history's page stained in the smog
                a nation fattening on its own starch
    grumbling back to the pit
                      in the guts of a car at the lights
      I spill into fantasy
              and eternity blasts
                      into scratches
                          I grow larger
                than the gods and wipe
          out the suburbs by the pond
                  knowing the library I know how to fall
        I steam with curses then wilt
    and freckle under the gleaming blade
                          Country lost in models
       of melting worlds

                  I awake
    to see my frame stripped of flesh
            its bloodied chalk like the cross
        of a flag
      my hips ooze
              with a blue, starry marrow
    the watts jag through my bed's
      baked quarry

                    I hear a gong or is it a moan
        is it the truth
                    telling me, from across the paddocks
                        telling me
        crammed onto the coast, onto the radio
who's telling me that a memory
            is the epoch's lonely fool

# Wander in &/Under

I wander in her woollen hat
snared in
                object world      of legs      dark
                          eyes
the city      becomes felt
                                  heels  click
  iron bent intomoss
              I am trodden    by
  a gull's filthy hotel    a self-conscious heart
            this spotted elephant
                          click
I wanteach   and   one    especially
                                  your
              flint   fried in    used oil
      a roasted   glebe
   I want      especially
                    this cold booth
        gladwrapped in
        skin
    every    object
                sex is    shackle
melodic      charge
      swooning over
   trodden      by conscious
     spurious motors
                prerogatives in
tend
   Iwander  her  forgotten hat
   I      dark eyes      your
    desire      beneath   a skirt
      like flakes struck  from  flint  like
    leathery spine      flakes

# Intertown

These old towns, these narrow streets, their museums,
all these modest, brightly painted homes strung together in intermittent successions,
these cobblestoned throats with throngs of lively people on their corners,
their productions of dance, culture, laughter,
showing how life can be lived, how it is made, I cannot recall
particular moments and I cannot grasp this intractable flow,
hundreds, thousands of reptilian streets, their lubricious sheen, their writhing,
and arthritic trees in plazas, and orange, cantankerous buses, oh,
that pretty church, oh, that kooky mural,
I'm a blank piece of meat clothed in aged shorts, in sweaty T-shirts,
I exert no effort, effort exhausts me,
what effort I've made got me here, and left me exhausted.

I see the range, I'm blessed with options,
with tour options, meal combos, with multi-coloured sarongs
and a selection of standard phrases,
in any instant I'll choose only one, can choose only one,
before I retire to the same, oily line, what time
do we eat? lunch, dinner, who knows?
In between these thoughts, more thoughts:
groups, relations, events that I wouldn't want to be part of,
that I'm not part of, but suddenly:
olive oil, balsamic vinegar, basil, god, *herbs*,
I get lost in them, want to be them, I want to be anything, I will do something,
tonight I'll be someone memorable, I'll do it right.
Thank god there's pop, funk, Prince,
I repeat these melodies mindlessly, in my mind,
when I speak I aim to suspend time, produce order,
but traffic moves silently in the distance, power is smoothed by distance,
these spikey cities studded with cheap jewels, eroding into streams of events, one after the other,
      I forget, I forget,

I will go home and reset, be loads happier,
make a place and relish it, become parochial, permanently.

All this fucking detritus, trash, this shit stacked up or flowing through vacant lots, ruined homes,
I look away but I'm a good person, my mother loves me,
I dream of declaring things spontaneously like a wild-haired artist. Everything's so spongey, spacey,
if I touch the side of my head there's a numbness between my fingertips and my consciousness.
Jesus, why am I still single?
I'm single in Japan, in Brazil, in Nigeria,
my head's in a little box somewhere in my mind, which is in a box inside a body somewhere in this town,
near the centre but not in the centre, a central edge, close to buses and the main attractions,
I show my eyes and my wallet gets me everywhere.
My love, my loves, where are you? People I've loved, who died,
and from somewhere, the toll of regatón and a large group of locals singing,
and at the table to my right they are marshalling the melodic fluid of fruits into wafer-thin glasses, god,
why did I say it that way?
Why do I say things?
Why did I? did it? Dithering and uncertain of what to claim,
my voices hide in the smog, swell with afternoon, the evening
is great for rhyme, dance, I can forget the day with a saggy sequel.
Have you seen the clock? what about the future?
I hear the dogs, I see their predicaments,
in the scatter of sounds I'm reminded of myself,
as if it were a kind of waking, each vision is a beginning,
while the paths of memory lead only to dream.
So much for an unfathomable life, a shining cross with plans for tomorrow!
I translate chemicals, I speak their accidents, I see opinions drooping into dialogue.
Occasionally, within the reverb, I can escape myself. Believe me,
the answers are small:
even after light years of travel, even if I could reach the end of light,
as this town dies, another would emerge, to the astonishment of the jungle
and for no reason.

## Isla Negra Ode

Has anyone been granted
as much joy as I have...?
 —Pablo Neruda

You were never going to be sad:
your desk arrived from the surf; you wrote a house with it
before sailing over those rubbery jungles of kelp
to the thatched origins of your words.

It's that briny smell, salty fists punching
when I walk across to your study.
You were exactly what I'd want to be
were I beginning again.

I'd still take most of it,
especially your marine lord, melted into horizon,
and your party for a wooden horse
with your hundreds of guests.

You lived with yours; I'd ask
my love to come with me to this house
of beetle, butterfly and pipe collections,
and colourful glass bottles mustered like so many empty souls.
I'd watch the footy on weekends.
I'd draft sonnets at one desk and odes at another.
I'd use up all of your green ink.

The sea would keep whispering, but
more of its inclinations, less
about the fish
and their fishermen.
And the land would weigh on my shoulders,

forever reminding me of a world
in which I no longer exist.

If you were ever frustrated
it was because the world opened itself to you
too often.
You painted lives with opal and coal
and when your battles fell down the fold
between this satellite and its sun,
you cloaked yourself in the night
to stroke your eternal cable.
You were never going to be sad.

No one would come to me but the seabirds.
I'd study your insects, your masks,
your antique globes and telescopes,
and each dormant relic would ignite like a flare
from some forgotten realm,
before returning to the darkness
between my body and what it wants.

# Storm

Samar, Philippines

The water was warm
as a childhood Christmas
before the storm slaughtered the afternoon.
The local kids were catching rides on all
kinds of stuff while I, more selective (lazier),
waited in the swoop
and lull for something bigger.

They were fooling around, rejuvenating the place
with their laughter—the chroma of the coast,
that nibbled shore—but the kids
didn't seem to notice what I couldn't ignore:
that monstrous, ashen structure spreading
across the sphere, snapping the shackles
of proportion.

When the kids realised they turned to paddle in,
leaving me alone with it.
They seemed to take an age to get to shore,
as if the beach were unmoored, and sailing
away from us. I wanted one last wave
but none emerged,
leaving me stranded in a rumbling tub.

Steadily feeding on the sea's
blackened bible, the storm began to fatten,
taunting me with incessant sketches of useless,
fractured swell. Each duck-dive sucked me
into shark-mind; the sets grew into behemoths,
and swallowed the universe into their whale-blue troughs.

I kept searching for an escape, for a ramp to the left
or right, I kept trying to turn, scanning
for sight of the coast's dwindling thread,
but my strokes had lost all purchase.
The conclusion was close, and already splitting apart.

At last it came (is this it? really?). It came,
broad-shouldered, shrouded in chop
and inflating into God. I can't let it pass,
I compress my apprehension
into a flurry of kicks—I'm lifted,
then dropped,
(a weightless instant's wilderness)
I'm thrown: spat race, pounding escape!

Soon my legs were grating over fringing reef
but then I was clambering out, gorging on air,
and the first rain drops splattered like bugs
on my relief, while the waxen sand
struggled to arc, arc
through the dent, the island
sinking into the future, and the end.

# Tierra Weather

*after Meredith Wattison*

all along the littoral, the boom
scatters shells across the lid
a sea lion breaks the surface
a graph blossoms into drops of flight

jewelled with grit
and physics, the dunes
levitate into pearl and chipped lead
stain with flux

the array's plucked from a ball of zero
and threaded through the needle
until the dunes consume the foam's

delicate, circular notes
fleeing, in a manic orchestra
the smashed necklace of your nerves

# Deep Dive

back to fall
once more into the mirrors
of our codes

                    the mooring rope
              cleaves the page in two

                                  swallowed in surf's fierce
                        suck we clash jostle we're thrown
                            we escape
                                        into a volcano's dead
                                      gullet

        damsel fish dash from crag sockets
                like cut packets
                  of pigment
                            deeper, deeper
                            until optics knot
                            with gasp

        we descend into compression
     beneath a slab's
         bulbous hug

                our lungs
                         mushroom
              out of pressure's grip
                      and rush in a streak of
                           wobbling monocles
              toward the limit
      where surf's hurled
into cliffs

                    we tuck into canyons
                    urchins fuzz quanta, faux-furry
                    in the Pacific belly
                    their frozen explosions of sting

                we slide
                        into narcosis
              on a slope old
           as reptile

                          sprouted from our lips
                rubber arteries strain
              to clasp aluminium
                              tubers full
of nitrogen seeds for the skull's
      sloppy loam: beads
            of pressurised *pop*
                  mixed with pumped hope
                                    (maskless,
       the world goes
              utero
      the floor's a gluey paste

                there's a cave's blazing
                      yellow innards, where
           consciousness
                  is
              charred)

  we inflate
  through the bones
  of another hoary mouth

       drips of sense
        trickle in to clear
         but death sharpens to
        a flight by a bluff's
      sallow stubble

        accelerating
    toward the bright, expanding
      like a bubble and grasping
          for anchor, he's
      scratched
 by the cone snail's spine
     a faint *prick* precedes
     an ecstatic throb then
     a scalding spike
     stresses the creature's
     insistence
        speech
    garbles into thrust
    and gulp

            in panic, the human
            claws at his face
      steals the air of the closest
    or

             pulls off his mask
                for briny mitts
                  to blur
                        while rocket ascent
                      pops a drum

                                        no exclamatory eel winding
                              easily through coral
                  no genial turtle gliding off
                          into the invisible next
        only depth, compressed
                        to a channel
                          where young time's
                        shed like a suit
                                  as the pale, wounded seal
                                              bullets skyward

# Hidden

The sierra has scoured off the sun,
leaving a chalky glow, an early dusk.

I've returned to remember
when you were waiting for me up there,

submerged in the chalky gloom
of our bedroom in the hacienda.

You were waiting for the heat
to press me back

into that room. Now, I'm camping
down by the brook,

where I'm huddled by the fire
beneath these fragile ribs of willow.

I'm camping alone, beneath thin leaves
hidden by as much as they hide.

Beneath these wispy ribs of willow
the stream's still the same,

hidden by as much as it hides,
shouting at silence and slowing into shade.

The brook's the same, brumal vein;
it's only when I head up the slope a little,

to where silences crouch in the shade,
on the trail we walked together,

only when I amble up the slope,
up past the meadow and the olive grove,

on the trail we walked,
I hear rock gulp, a ridge's looming fin.

Beyond the meadow and the olive grove,
a looming fin slicing air,

rocks gulping, then:
What have I done?

Fin slicing air,
my heart went stale.

*What have I done?*
I stumble on the way back down.

My heart cracks
when I fall

on the way back to camp;
reaching out,

falling,
a needle from the churqui's trunk

—as I'm reaching out—
spears my palm.

A churqui's long wooden needle;
tonight could be the sort of night,

nursing my stinging, purple palm,
that my eyes suddenly meet the puma's.

Tonight could be the night
that I need to keep writing,

but my gaze wanders and meets a puma's
in the purple of the penumbra.

I need to keep writing regardless,
to give my utterance a little

of the penumbra's last dye,
our slender scar's dying light.

I need to give my writing
to our sandy grey trail,

the slender scars of our footprints
bloody with squashed ticks.

Along that grey, powdery trail,
I'm hidden by as much as I hide, a squished

tick's ink on your arm
on that last, summer afternoon.

You are hidden by as much as you hide,
your shadow sliding over the rapids,

you are that last afternoon
I've come back to find, but

strange phrases stream over the rapids
and curl into a lonely dish.

I've come back to find the mosquitoes
subsumed in the river's never-ending noise.

Swirling in autumn's basin,
billowing hordes of mosquitoes

and saturating, never-ending noise...

## Wagga to Coast

So, what happens is—what happens
  when you come out this way—the town
    sort of dribbles
      out, it sort of whimpers into zip,
then you're flying over slopes
         or through them,
  your music's playing, you dip in & out of it,
your hands are easy on the wheel, signs are ballooning & slapping,
  the land's velvety, shimmering, braingreen,
   you remember something your mum said about it,
  the sun's still low so winter's long,
          spindly shadows fall
      from the eucalypts,
slow drafts ruffle the fields and shake free
  droplets of light.
      You see scatters
 of austere trunks, too—their looming
wilt,
  lonely in a patch or climbing a rise,
occasional choirs pattering about in a huddle—
   everything's very matt, very earnest.

  It's only when huddles of rock
         pop up in places—it's only then
  that you can imagine getting out of the car—
   stopping by the side of the road, getting out
       and scrambling about for a while,
  feeling your legs awaken,
       push against your thinking—but
you pass a few semis with sheep stuffed into trailers,
   their greasy wool bulging through the grills,

and some of them are looking at you, their eyes black as pits.
You decide to keep going for now.

                        You change CDs, juggling the wheel
    with their silly cardboard cases (less
    clumsy than an algorithm)…

After Canberra it's pretty clear that things are getting fluffier,
        more reflective, the grass spilling over
                        eroded enjambments,
  and out towards Braidwood the gums will stand up to you,
           showing off their shining
                    stripes and burgundy muscles,
overwhelming you with all the gloom
of the bush behind them,
      with all the myriad roots of their kin behind them,
    going back so far,
          going back all the way, their gnarled,
      leaden bulk, their staggered stories,
   and what a lover once shouted at you
      from within the furrows of her form.

    After all that, what you're coming to—
  changing one hand on the wheel for the other—
              one alternating with the other—
what you're coming to is the end of the journey,
but before it happens, you start
      to happen, you start to occur,
                  clusters of fern
  greeting you with verdant explosions
as you begin the descent to the coast, they're
    almost like feather dusters soaked in late
                  light, almost like downy

                        bedding in which you could rest
after your hardships on the thinner roads,
            those thinner roads further back, when you were
    lurching through those wild, woolly zones
                                    crammed with tomato timber,
those cedars thrashing their heads together, meshing
their heads together,
                the millions of leaves of their heads
                        meshed together,
   scraping, slashing each other,
millions of sharp, oily leaves
                        chopping up the lumens, the gusts
                    buffeting the remnants of your day,
collapsing your life into a lone, sorry line
                snailing towards whatever it was
                                you were searching for
            and hoping to touch.

So the descent
        into the ferny protrusions
   of the coast
    is a relief,
            and you sigh
                    with crisp forest.
            You haven't forgotten,
you were coming this way for a reason,
                        there's something to be said for racing
            past the spongy floodplains
                        and the turn-offs
    to the entrances
of national parks.
Now there's a paler sky, there's an old farm shed
                at a corner

with a roof going xanthous in the slant.
        What's going on is that you're finding the end,
            then you've reached the end of a gravelled culdesac
                                    by the beach,
    with tubby rosellas picking at titbits
                        over by the car park,
with scatters of banksia buns
                and creamy grey gums knotted up
                          with childhood times
            and those times with other times,
      with saw-leaf and bird fiddle, beak clap and belly squabble,
their fingers extended or closing a little
                      but thicker than fingers
                          and clumped, lumped
                into the hands of hundreds
                      of careful, immovable custodians
          sheltering your conclusions
as the day is sucked into stars.

\*

In the lunar
            mode of the following
                        dawn
with those quartz holes
      through which almost any
                        thought
                  can escape,
  you'll float back to the lull
                  of that long line
and the way the paddocks rolled out for you,
            with certain trees pointing,
   and the part where you turned
                  and left it—all of it
      in terms of squinting
                  and glimpsing the watch—
and the paddocks will morph into dreams—
                  you'll peer into them
         as if atop a cooling parabola
before it falls into the sea.
                  Soon the series
will stop repeating
         and the waves, with the whole coast watching,
will fill with the bloodied milk
      of a split sun.

# Field Notes

# Fade, Into

When I arrived, it was hard to believe that my eyes weren't playing tricks on me. That first, flooded moment—

>(an enormous gorge, rising sharply to the limits of sight)

>(stony villages fringing the rise)

>(the green upon green reiterations)

>(ridge lines retreating like stormy swell into the distance)

Who'd have thought that life could occur amidst such steepness, such drama? Who could imagine such a stage? It seemed fantastical, and it certainly started out that way: I felt myself exhale and relax into infinite volume. Language, even mind, seemed of questionable value.

\*

Why describe a place in terms of how you first see it? As if the first impression is literally the im*press*ion, after which I'm forever marked.

(now, a slowly-rising sense that I've written of this previously, in almost exactly the same way…)

\*

At a dinner with some locals, he asked if I'd ever been to a place like this before. No, I don't think so, I said. Though what I wanted to say was, *Yes, I have, many times, in reflections, in sketches, in the spaces around reflections and sketches…* Not to mention the fact there is no other world, that we all live in the conditions of this one…

Though in a way such a question will never have an answer. What he really wanted to know was: how does this place make me *feel?* Or: how far does it rest beyond what you can say?

It filled me entirely at first, all my thinking was bound to the steep slopes in front of my balcony. But after a week or so I found that the slopes had withdrawn, or flattened slightly. What I saw was no longer unspeakably stunning; it was simply *there*, like the chair on my balcony, the pen on my desk.

*

A lot is to do with the people who live here: they work, they travel to other villages to see friends; they like some neighbours, avoid others. Their lives thread the topography with an urban regularity; their meandering stories seem to unsettle that gigantic canvas of sky-mountain-forest, to push it back.

Though 'push' isn't the right word; it's more to do with submerging the image in a shallow pool...

At this juncture the temptation is to lapse back into that lament—for places I've lost, for those I've visited but have not really *seen*, etc. It's true, after all, that new places seem to recede gradually from view the longer I stay in them. But the deeper question is about *what* they recede into. That fading away...

(into what? into void?)

*

At another dinner, one of my companions spoke of the recent death of her mother. On her way to the dinner, she had gathered a small bunch of Pyrenean irises and left them on the grave. Walking back to my room after the meal, I found myself looking for their sprawling purple petals by the road's edge. That it was near midnight and I could barely see the ground meant little: there was the conversation at dinner, and the irises for a new friend's mother.

*

There are various ways to conceive it, but for now it seems best to say that, in apparently 'receding' from the very frontier at which sight almost erupts into the rest of me, these places have actually been released. Freed of my desperate senses, they are allowed to venture off—

(unmoored in a pool, the image drifts)

Having recovered their freedom, places then seem to progress by tilling and unsettling the earth like ponderous, glacial ledges. Amidst all the surprises they upturn, I find myself looking closer. There are crumbled rocks and ochre powders and shredded stems and branches and pottery chips through the sticky loam—

I find myself walking in slowly-expanding circles, fixated on the emergence of things. At other times, though, I'm not concentrating on the ground or the distance at all. As more days pass, I am still less overcome by the size of the valley or by the way that, towards evening, lightning appears to dangle momentarily over the highest peaks. This occurs more or less at the same time as

*

(by ruined walls that must date back to the Romans)

(by a crumbling hermitage on a hill's forehead)

Objects become orientation rather than spectacle.

Certain tracks have emerged, from my room to elsewhere, for particular routes and directions. And because of these patterns there's more of a looseness between my thoughts and how I take in what surrounds them. I move less randomly, but more freely; certain compositions—

    (slope and ravine)

    (cottage and a trail of poplars to the brook)

—have dissolved, or at least withdrawn slightly. Beauty, its bold shock, evaporates and leaves me on the fertile ground it occupied.

(various channels, rivulets, nets, etc., rather than a single, irresistibly magnetic surface)

Take, for example, the house far above the highest meadow, almost hidden by sub-alpine stands of birch and pine—

(then, considering how I might reach it)

(or discarding the notion because

## The Trees

are probably the largest selves in the forest

but they are also the most obvious:
forthright, upright, they accord immediately
with the human vertical, and as they grow
they wrinkle;
when cut, they weep.
They could be the cousins
of our ideals: calmer, grander,
wiser.

Look at them gathered, their patient multitudes.
Beneath tinnitus, beneath breathing,
their webs hum with verb.
What the highway whines they dispel, gently as listening.

You can walk among them, you can touch
or talk to them, they won't run.
Some you can even climb, but others
will tremble with your weight—then,
as their arms give way, the sound
of frozen flesh torn apart.

Slowly they slide behind one other.
Slowly, the screen folds and unfolds;
knowledge congeals into multiple singulars.

Can you see their stripes? Gnarled furrows of space,
wound cables of time.
They yearn for the steps to Being.
Their greatest, collective achievement: the shape of gravity.

'Commitment'
is meaningless: they might waver,
but they'd sooner die than depart.

Reaching, shedding their becoming,
scaling the tower of Being.

Gradually, the forest expands into bract-cumulus;
in its billows and crannies it creates universes.
Here are the trees, guardians of dimensions.

Through the crystal lattice of time, light cracks.

## Old World

It's certainly true that all the precipitation and the rich,
glacial loam produce an incredibly verdant profusion;
sometimes it can verge on absurdity, on a green so intense it almost screams:
super-saturated with faith in plenty,
stalks, thickets, leas can almost leak out of themselves into luxuriant
abstractions and blur
into floods of spinach and jade.

But you also notice how much simpler the ecology is—
as the palette's almost monochromatic,
the flora and fauna aren't as various;
in any segment of woodland you won't find a fraction of the diversity,
and then those stands themselves are but patches
in quilts of barley and wheat,
with villages huddled like cays in their blonde, swaying oceans,
and silver frames of birch along the roads,
like the cliffs of distant coasts.
Even the hills rise gently,
then dwindle before ever really imposing themselves—not to mention
the fact that it all disappears each winter,
when the plenitude gets corralled into a void
covered with russet wrapping.

So there's an alarming simplicity to the territory:
it's so harmless,
very little can belittle you,
and what there is can be ordered into neat categories.
It makes you realise that many of the early settlers
must have expected similar simplicity
when they boarded ships for the New Worlds:
acres of velvety grasses, with gentle hummocks and rivulets,

and an earth that, when you walked on it,
would immediately depress beneath the shape of your shoe, while,
no matter their size or structure, the woods
around you, right after you'd entered them,
would promptly vanish by a farm or a lane—and
for the most part, around your plans and their postulates,
if not human noises, then
taught warbles, precise chirps,
petite pockets of silence: nothing too raucous
or too vast.

That *disgust* they felt, then,
when the great brown land went beyond them,
when it banished the rain and refused domestication
and struck back with heat and snake
and spear,
might have been kin to their hatred of women
who pressed for suffrage,
or of those people coming in from the edges,
who didn't seem nearly as disgusted or appalled.

Here on this green island,
with its constant showers, its submissive soil,
I can whistle to the modest melodies of wee birds
in the copse, I can see the roots of my history
in a facile geography, and the error
in appealing to its soggy basis.

# Sutherland

Most of the terrain was scooped out,
leaving malachite lumps of muscle
and exposed outcrops of claret-
grey marrow.

Anything substantially vertical or colourful
was taken. What's left
is sewn into the open
by a single wren—

who's he calling,
across this slumbering, swollen globe?

Perpetually damp;
even in mid-summer, it's mud-bogged, water-logged.
It needs to dry out, to unleash itself

but lochs insist, with their belligerent feet,
on low, leaden skies.

A figure on a summit could be seen for miles;
the one who sees owns nothing
but a name for the place.

## Upon the Tongue of a Valley's Enormous Mouth

… the gumtree reaches back and out, bathed in the earth's mineral radiance.
—John Anderson

It's as if separate floods of eucalyptus had crashed into one another,
were colliding with one another,
two great, heaving forests bulging and buckling on impact,
before they were frozen solid.

Many trees were pushed to the edges
and are about to fall into the ravines—suspecting something
of the chaotic events which led to this precarious situation,
we could surmise that they have hurled—that
they are hurling—out their branches
in all directions in desperate attempts
to hold on, to anchor themselves.

In fact, after examining the cliff and the bush behind it,
it does seem as if everyone, from mallee ash to blue gum, was in the process of grasping
before they were all frozen, or caught in the act,
so that their peach and lemon blossoms are gasps,
like mouths surfacing; they bobble in the gusts
(but their other purpose could be to explore the façade
like periscopes, to scan its great cavern so their trees can determine
how long they'll have to wait underneath).
Those blossoms say something smooth as a salmon-hued trunk
but incomprehensible as liquid quartz.

At any rate, it's probably fair to assume that the gums were going somewhere
when trapped by the slick wrap of my sight.
In their incarceration, either they are waiting patiently or they're slowly dying.
At first glance, they appear to be doing the latter—shedding bark
and rasping puffs of currawongs and cockatoos

when I snap or stumble.
Their only hope of rescue seems to be in tinkling
splashes of leaves,
or in streaks of alabaster and ochre
along flame-scarred flanks.

But being locked in my heavy, gelatinous film
could amount to nothing more than an electric shock
in the eon of a eucalypt's vibration.
I like to think that they're waiting, or inching towards an escape,
reaching for a slit in the field
that we're too fast to catch.

yellow:

If you observe the calyx of what I think is the white daffodil—the one with the snowy petals and the buttery protrusion of cups within (I'm not exactly sure what they're called, but I know I *should* know—

there's a kind of lyrical imperative that the poet be an expert on nomenclature, as if the correct name is the capacity of a thing, as if the name is what a thing must become, as if these daffodils—these ones, here—would shrivel up without their names)

if you observe closely, you'll see even smaller buds within the golden cups

: some of these buds have erupted into tiny flowers of their own, while older remnants have accreted around the fringes into a heavy, brain-like clump, which causes the daffodil to droop.

: in fact, the youngest daffodils have no yellow cup at all, but rather a thinner, white one.

: so, between the purely white daffodils and those bulging with buttery brain, between a name and the innermost, innermost bud, daffodils becoming—

# Branch

that old branch, crackling

through the gargle and glimmer of the calls
the looped cells,

the glassy fallen light, frothing wattle
and brown snakes pouring
out of nowhere

it divides into crinkling legs and kinks
through compressed dimensions, tilts

and rolls
into a twisted, neuronal lexicon

but its tendency to trip over
covert zones
to slip into foregrounds and
belie its own, sprawling presence, signals
like a rising temperature

a confusion, a swarm of brail data
pouring from radiant nerves

leaving trains of parasites across the pupils—
what we peer beyond to find

frond, burst pods, the fine
skeleton

of a flipped leaf and
somewhere, hopefully, the dull blaze
of an escarpment

with drowsy totems dotted
along a baked track

# Some More Thoughts on the Rainforest

There are the obvious points, like how dense it is, how entangled it is.
On a map: its scattered emerald freckles down the right flank of the continent;
after all the fires and the clear-felling, it persists in fragments,
where the land reaches to catch the weather, induce a rupture,
soaking the ferment and the last refuges of Antarctic Beech.

Unlike Peru, say, Australia wouldn't look much different without it
and few of us would notice if it disappeared.
But imaginations and their stories would be devastated;
no longer enclaves packed with every idea made real,
the Dividing Ranges would harden into the crag of a phrase.

It might be remarkable precisely because of its scarcity, its absence;
like any baroque, its complexity is extraordinary.
It's Australian camp, all verdant extravagance, dancing in defiance
of gridded plains of ash-greyness. Hardly anything's straight,
there's no sacrosanct model, the fig slowly
strangles its heritage to fatten
into the post-modern; any position
is entangled with others, a subject is an object,
or another subject, a trans-ject;
the struggle for survival is also a shared intimacy with death:
individuation will lead, at some point, to its donation.

At any rate, it's all or nothing, it *begins* and it *ends*,
it rarely peters out. Inside, there's no outside
save for a few, stubborn slivers of sky.
But despite its density, the gaps are innumerable;
after you cross the gloom of a gorge,
the sun can spill through an aperture and snag in the leaves
until they flare like luminescent fruits.

It drips and flops and creaks,
when a breeze passes through, it ruffles its sage and kelly feathers.
It could be the ultimate chameleon: from a distance, it's a single organism
contorted with its own coherence; from within,
it differentiates ceaselessly, until you can see the cells of your own name
beneath a tree's flaking skin.

And who could forget the vines of the puppet masters,
who funnel the lot into shaking poems?
Thatching copses into dancing nodes,
they disguise their archetypes in melody history.
What lyrebirds make is code for what made them,
the key's in wanting,
when the forest speaks itself, and imitation invents inhabitation:
calls are materials, desire is a mechanism with seeds in the soil,
the production of replicas, recombinant reproduction,
not to mention reduction, a range reduced to a line,
or the field's contrary insistence—induction, no plane
or point but sky-thin bowls,
in which what is possible might find itself bound
to what is not, limbs entangled, mulched
and sweaty,
art is in what it wants, its symphonic mess.

South-East

# Hinterland

first the                mag
       nificent stone slapped
                         across the basin
                    /
   (acacia brushing the gusts

leaking shadows glow
          asking the pastures) then
                      to play
                   /
               my turn
     to balance on a thermal dizzy
                    with eagle
rivulets of vineyards and scattered avocado

                       groves
       glints in a rift a single I'm joining
                \
              with the slit gulps
         in a triptych itdoeswhatitdoes
                    unwinds to punt
                   bumbling etceteras
                       —into topoi
        chunky plumes of broccoli
   gangs of innumerable gums
      \
       stooping to draw the groove
            the canopy's hazy scales
                   the cusp of
    weight fluvial wake coiled tight
          around solemn

                                        magnets they mash
                            paints into jazz from
                                        \ \
                            here to the image of it
                        from the brink to what skirts it
                a serpent's smouldering eye blinks
                    ) )
    with west          I can see her path         but I lose track
                            of what she might
                                        do when I step
                    out and fill my intention
                        with curling canyon
                    )
    strings of creeks r
                    attling b
                            ack to the coast

# Black Rocks

                                              the coal bones  
                    groan amongst the green  
                                thrush the pools  
      mouth the scorched calls  
    of the fuzzed buds it's  

      wallaby time os-  
            prey time to  
        step  
      into the on  
               shore  
to trip on a law be-  
tween tiff & low  
        tide I/m bounding  

        off to fern country  
            thump  
       & thud through toasted  
     mobiles joking in the jade  
              squirt my dumb  
                  glint the shivers  

          of river glass  
               slice  
     & sieve it radix relaxed  
     into bank all my  
           feeding my  
        loaming neither  
     here        nor hair  
          shooot! (whip

                    box) steaks
              & knots of
                   cumulus over the lemon
             collar I/swirl
       pearl
             shell my plate
                         python waits
                                        pity
                               the mice the chicks
                   out for a stroll
                tuned tubular

                    mandibula huge &
                              notsosized m/y shrill
              turkey pulls the frills
                         to the dribble behind the
                               dune where I/mown/ed
                    by iridescent umbra
                                til it's chopped

## Late World, Humid

  that fire shape
       fractured into brush, shimmer
              begging beach, beech sprayed
         with moonglow
             chopped out quick
     -ly by the northern beat
       in a bit
          nursing out loud, that
      peaked lyre
       straightest
pine who, cunning crook
      goes woop, copiously
     copious laurel grafting tune, grinding tune
   to waft, where
        emergent adders rough apple, the breasted
 buttons swallow wedges, a rare yellow
        belly walks the sticks
            talks the end
          they all pick the sites, it ends
        on the sides, their
   clashed out curve, underground sun
        sews dusk with sound, silence
     with flocks
  of delirious leaves'
     early loom, their fickle
      jolt bou-
     quet, this star
       caught in mist
    it dries tiny and rays
       it croaks
    stinks, some

                                facts slip out
                                        and feed
        that heavy west

# Verge

The night's worn down by the ridge
until it breaks apart and morning unrolls
like a chapter along the street.

Sprigs screw into sand and
salmon fat ribbons, strap
my body to the glass limit.

A canyon's intentions
are dwarfed by a lanky huntsman's
endless jaw, all pitch cavities

and stripped flash, entombed heat

pouring into that frothing, titanic stomach
stitched with a ruined castle's tuber,
its ponderous cycles of cicada and verge

until the canopy cracks with blaze.
The sodden pot's wrenched free.
Gumnuts mime the chorus,

sandstone and iron-
stone shiver with rubble. The cleft
awaits, its slumbering muscle

twitching with the residue of
the current that cut
through hunks of bush

to scrawl its name upon the lens,
back when billows nestled and chattering
magnified to ache, or swoon.

# Song of the Wandering Cat

*1.*

you've run from the lowland's crazy harvest
    run to the ravine's azure loft
          resting on this idle rim
           the song breathing hard within you
  resting
  a song is breathing
                        the wind sneaks up
        sneaks up on the shoulders of the silence
  sneaking up
    asking, aaasking—only the mmm
    the merest tip, near-white, its slightest asking, "Who?

who?" Then: "WHO?"
                "WHO ARE YOU?"

                        before laying its woolly
          blanket over sleeping slab

at rest you're rolling mesas coated in onyx syrup
                    you're on the brim of One
            in the margins of measure

      you've never known who but wants re-elongate you, you glare presence

                    oozing this sweet honey
you're a child of the thumping paw
                              the rolling canto
                    the pure phrase
                                        your tail's a serpent
            it follows you breezily through altitudes
                                            eternity's at your back
                                    the land is brittle
                                                as rat fossil

*2.*

or the shape is a log glinting with moss
and you're lost in lamp, swiping at tinges
of spider and tick
in which case you're a frail, spluttering orb
                      an organism shrinking amidst the honeyed-smoke
                                                of fried almonds

                    but this melody keeps returning
                    until you purr with its pattern

                earth is certainty
                      your body is mercurial
                      relocation
                                          you're seeping back to jewel potential
                                                      a smile in the night's pupil
          who
              ever
        might approach will trip
      on your knitted edicts
                            shredded by synonym
                            lashed by saliva strings, your fierce
                            gristle-horn fight!
but the song stops again
you are cured meat beside a mossy log

3.

>*Now:*
>Miles from a sign, compacting conjecture
>>into a torrent's punch, or
>sting and spider pike, or
>>drill and tick guts.

>You're at weather's mercy;
>>your tail's a blind serpent.
>You are slug frequency heavy,
>>clumsier than speech.

>You are still seeking the song.

>>*Now:*
>>At rest you are rolling knolls coated
>>in coal syrup.

>>Your paws know better. Signal squeezed into claws,
>>into your weald of teeth: all sense ends in *shred*.

>>At rest you're the rolling hills,
>>or you're relocating mercurially.

>>Any snap, any rustle is
>>*strike*.

*Now:*
You are land-beat, sprig-limbed:
  in flight you shed semantic cloaks;
    your crown is carved in adolescent stone.
You are far from here and always;
you're at peace here and always, kill: chorus ruptures;
    potent and nervous, vibe's zapped with swerves,
 porous as the heaviest.
This song you are, still.

# Cabo Polonio

A morning's sweet, windless limp,
a young grey life ends in a crease
ringed by crimped grit.

Later: petals crammed between jubes of succulent.

*

The shelf's split to the crux.
The terms are lax, despite their bleeding iron.
An outcrop's lumpen strewn
echoes buried cerebrum, recalls an Incan-
Polynesian construction, a tectonic weave
in a clear, floating egg.

*

Soon the cries arrive, hit the rim,
smooth slab stuffed with lightning, but shucked
slick drains
out to pasture.

Or a lichen melange, a chorus of damp blubber
and their chubby pups,
then a seagull's lone, snowy point:

the sign of death is a limp neck.

*

Back of that heap there's a sunset
but what don't we know of it?
Its broken box, its tilted meadow.
A rock's pulse dries into arcs
of gravel graphics.

The lichen tips:
the roof tipping into mustard—

gleaming terracotta sleds below the surface,
torn geometries fuse into glitchy sentence.

## Laguna

The eye is in the mind,
    molten focus,
    grassed then hurried
with shiver,
    bristled with talk.
    To touch it
is a yarn, an element
    of fable augurs
    the drizzle,
each drop slips into a quick
    little mouth, busy copper
    pops in the Central Desert,
where words carve the laws
    of their origin, let poiesis
    ferment, or rest
in the strobes
    at the edges of vowels.

    After, scraps of light
blow down the valley to sketch
a decrepit bed, the eye
    lost on a somnambulant talus.
    Wet conifers knit
plains of thorny scrub
to slogans of bleached-
    white blossom.
    The angle is released from the earth
into the nerves, which melt
into icy strings
    down the saddle,
    a tome in trickles
like the skeletons
    of migrating songs.

# South-East

the fist is a mulled
squall beneath
the cerulean half

lid crumbles and
streaks to hug the rest
trembles and hauls
itself up onto pillars

of vine and gnarled
bellow
weather-
beaten and littoral a bit

moist in the cockles what
can't flex snaps
the corner's drenched on
and on it flukes

and gusts cussing
about curious
about the instant
intent on roll and
the pour

into grassy circular
verdigris riverine
gurgling and rills
beneath the churn into
streams

of charismatic
topography
until the squeeze
of the periphery where

it all links
together again a ring
cast thinner than light
around a vast

open verging
on volume before
it grows hazy
shivering and
rucks

## Partial, & Remorse

—what we're left with here is a hand
in another (the close

examination of a knuckle): what
happens next, what

happened now—these blurred
                                        wrens darting
into the scrub

behind us—inside us (in the wind
swept channel, the whipped

cream of a torrent's toes
                              retreating
                              the available possibilities in the tatters

the gingery hind-leg of a
                              camera as it chases
an oyster catcher gliding above the bow)—

back then (carving my lungs from the water)
when I clung to you

like a barnacle on the hull: gestation
of a muscle you didn't want

timbre of the flattest peaks
                                circuit of the smallest wing—
what happens now, in your murky wake?

(& the vault's searing slap:
winded in the thump, the delicious beasts

of the ultra-
           marine multi, their hooking
spoon) coughed spume
                      torn

and ionic, coming up for air (where are you?)
breaching that wary void
                      corrugated

                      glimmers, the ecstatic
noun of a night's suffocated face, seated
                            amongst bells:
                            amongst hands

my feet eaten by a magma
slithering below the veneer of the sand is
                          needing

what I need, further & prior to any of this: your
relentless desire—the design
                    of a coast

one waiting for the other's
                  wake—an other's
unwavering voyage

# Wollombi

Hauling my phantom across the fields,
my voices lilt in the anonymous hours.
Summer sweats with crumbs of spring.

A lake trembles in the breeze
in a bruised, shallow valley
with a worn polish of pasture.

Woodlands stitch the sky.
Orange-flecked boulders
are strewn between wood and word

like ancient marks of punctuation.
After silence,
cicadas rattle my engine, flatten Yengo;

the will disappears. Over the wrangled fence
of the badlands, down into the wound,
solar flares stripe a furry rump, a dappled patch

choked by pine clutch—
there you are, wisping into a premonition.
Entombed in the glade, what I expect

bumps into what I feel.
The ground thrives with sugar ants.
The grass is greener over your grave.

# Notes

The epigraph for 'In Memory' is from *The Visible and the Invisible* (1964), translated by Alphonso Lingis.

'This is what you have done for me' refers to the artist John Olsen (1928-).

'Coastal, as in Galactic' was written in response to Joy Harjo's 'Bird' (from *In Mad Love and War*, 1990). The poem contains a line adapted from Michael Jackson's 'Off the Wall' (on *Off the Wall*, 1979) and a phrase adapted from John Ashbery's 'The System' (in *Three Poems*, 1972): "… certain younger spectators felt that all had already come to an end, that the progress toward infinity had crystallized in them, that they in fact were the other they had been awaiting, and that any look outward over the mild shoals of possibilities that lay strewn about as far as the eye could see was as gazing into a mirror reflecting the innermost depths of the soul."

'Feed' is an alternative version of 'Mapa' by Murilo Mendes (in *Poemas*, 1930).

'I Love Mine' is a response to 'My Country' by Dorothea Mackellar (in *The Closed Door*, 1911).

The epigraph for 'Isla Negra Ode' is from 'Autumn Testament' (in *Estravagario*, 1958).

'Sutherland' is the traditional territory of Clan Sutherland, a Highland Scottish clan from which my mother's family are descended.

The epigraph for 'Upon the Tongue of a Valley's Enormous Mouth' is from 'love, the cartographer's way' (in *the forest set out like the night*, 1995).

# Acknowledgements

I'm indebted to Peter Boyle, Berndt Sellheim, Meredith Wattison and David Musgrave for their invaluable feedback, and to David for having me back.

My thanks to the editors of the following publications, where earlier versions of many of these poems were published: *Bareknuckle Poet*, *Blackbox Manifold* (UK), *Clade Song* (USA), *Contra Equus Niveus* (USA), *Cordite*, *Griffith Review*, *HEAT*, *Island*, *Marrickville Pause*, *Meanjin*, *Overland*, *Peril*, *Pink Cover Zine*, *Plumwood Mountain*, *Poetry Salzburg* (Austria), *Rabbit*, *Shearsman* (UK), *Social Alternatives*, *The Best Australian Poems 2016*, *The Crows in Town: 2017 Newcastle Poetry Prize Anthology*, *The Dreaming Machine* (Italy), *Southerly*, *Tinfish* (USA) and *WOB*.

'In Memory' won the 2016 Gwen Harwood Poetry Prize.

I wrote this book with the generous support of Griffith University's Centre for Social and Cultural Research, along with residential fellowships from Arteles Creative Center (Finland), the Atlantic Center for the Arts (under Master Artist Joy Harjo; USA), Centre d'Art i Natura (Spain), and Djerassi Resident Artists' Program (USA).

The poems were drafted on the lands of the following First Nations, with gratitude: Bundjalung, Darkinung, Diaguita, Dharug, Gubbi Gubbi, Guaraní, Jagera, Kulin, Mapuche, Mohican, Ngarrindjeri, Quandamooka, Rapa Nui, Timucua, Tupinambá, Yadhaigana, Yaruwu, Yugambeh and Waray.

Milton Keynes UK
Ingram Content Group UK Ltd.
UKHW052015310723
426074UK00027B/759